Chinchillas

by Vanessa Black

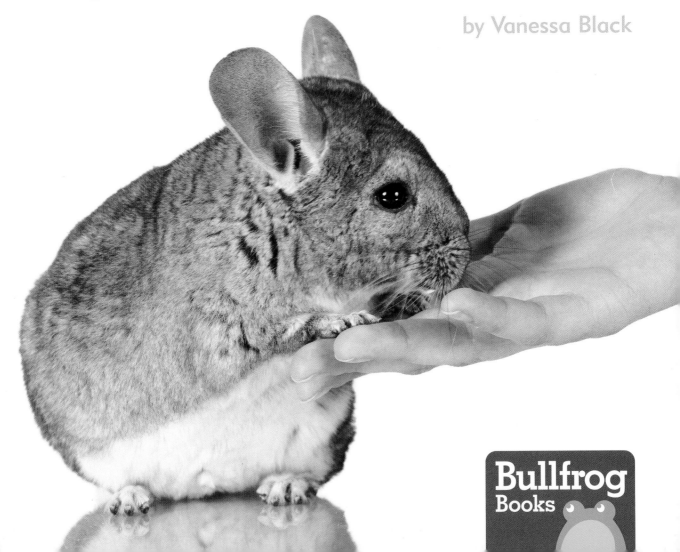

Bullfrog Books

Ideas for Parents and Teachers

Bullfrog Books let children practice reading informational text at the earliest reading levels. Repetition, familiar words, and photo labels support early readers.

Before Reading

- Discuss the cover photo. What does it tell them?
- Look at the picture glossary together. Read and discuss the words.

Read the Book

- "Walk" through the book and look at the photos. Let the child ask questions. Point out the photo labels.
- Read the book to the child, or have him or her read independently.

After Reading

- Prompt the child to think more. Ask: What do you need to take care of a chinchilla? Would you like one as a pet?

Bullfrog Books are published by Jump!
5357 Penn Avenue South
Minneapolis, MN 55419
www.jumplibrary.com

Library of Congress Cataloging-in-Publication Data

Names: Black, Vanessa, author.
Title: Chinchillas / by Vanessa Black.
Other titles: Bullfrog books. My first pet.
Description: Minneapolis, MN: Jump!, Inc., [2017]
Series: My first pet | Audience: Ages 5–8.
Audience: K to grade 3. | Includes bibliographical references and index.
Identifiers: LCCN 2016022399 (print)
LCCN 2016027194 (ebook)
ISBN 9781620315491 (hardcover: alk. paper)
ISBN 9781624964978 (ebook)
Subjects: LCSH: Chinchillas as pets—Juvenile literature.
Classification: LCC SF459.C48 B53 2017 (print)
LCC SF459.C48 (ebook) | DDC 636.935/93—dc23
LC record available at https://lccn.loc.gov/2016022399

Editor: Kirsten Chang
Book Designer: Michelle Sonnek
Photo Researcher: Michelle Sonnek

Photo Credits: All photos by Shutterstock except: Adobe Stock, 11, 22; Alamy, 16, 22; Bree Wrolson, 14–15, 23tl; Getty, 20–21; Newscom, 5, 23br; Superstock, 12–13, 18–19.

Printed in the United States of America at Corporate Graphics in North Mankato, Minnesota.

Table of Contents

A New Pet

Jax wants a soft pet.

He gets a chinchilla!

Chins are social.

They do not like
to be alone.

5

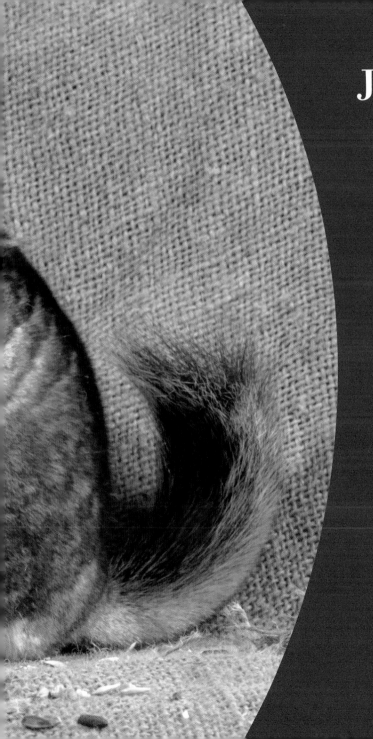

Jax's sister gets one, too.

Now the chins can play.

Ivy holds Lex.

She is gentle.

She does not
hold him tightly.

Tony feeds Dot.
He feeds her pellets.

pellets

He feeds her hay.
He gives her water.

11

Chins need
a lot of room.

They like to jump.

They like to run.

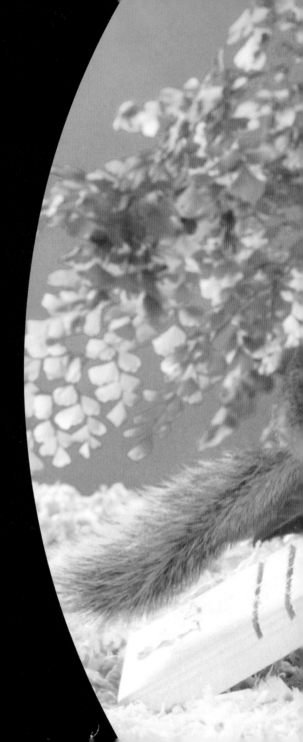

exercise wheel

14

Nut Nut has
an exercise wheel.

She loves it!

She runs and runs.

Amy cleans Zola's cage.

It is big!

Ted gives Sid
a bowl of dust.

Sid rolls in it.

It cleans his fur.

dust

Chinchillas are fun pets!

What Does a Chinchilla Need?

water bottle
Chinchillas need glass water bottles. They will chew plastic ones.

hut
Chinchillas need a place to hide.

shavings
Line a chinchilla's cage with aspen or shredded paper shavings; other kinds can hurt their lungs.

hay
Give chinchillas timothy hay to eat. It is good for their teeth and digestion.

Picture Glossary

exercise wheel
A wheel made
for small pets
to run on.

pellets
A mix of crushed
up food made into
small chunks.

gentle
Calm and kind;
not rough.

social
To enjoy being
around other
people and
animals.

Index

To Learn More

Learning more is as easy as 1, 2, 3.

1) Go to www.factsurfer.com

2) Enter "petchinchillas" into the search box.

3) Click the "Surf" button to see a list of websites.

With factsurfer.com, finding more information is just a click away.